101 Ways That Show
He's Worth It
👍 👍 👍

101 Ways That Show He's Worth It

👍 👍 👍

Girl, be smart and wise up now!

Wendt Francoise

PARTRIDGE
A Penguin Random House Company

To order additional copies of this book, contact
Toll Free 800 101 2657 (Singapore)
Toll Free 1 800 81 7340 (Malaysia)
orders.singapore@partridgepublishing.com

www.partridgepublishing.com/singapore

Foreword

This list was initially drafted as a guide for my personal use. It is a compilation of actual gestures and actions done to me by my ex-boyfriends plus scenes witnessed by me of my father and brothers, male friends, male cousins, uncles, and close friends' boyfriends and husbands.

A real man's worth to his woman is his love expressed through his actions. Every man shows his love in different manners. This is a list of actions that touched my heart and the hearts of my female loved ones and friends.

My wish is to be able to share some of these insights with fellow sisters who may be confused or lost or blinded by lust / love and crave another opinion or voice to give them more clarity and some balance in their love lives. And if you are falling in love for the first time, then this book will hopefully provide new perspectives for you on how great a man's love can be, if he truly cherishes you.

I sincerely hope that this book will be of some use to you in the present moment and whenever you need to refer to it.

101 Ways That Show
He's Worth It
👍👍👍

1.   He's worth it if he lets you be who you are without forcing you to change or become that other person he wants you to be. This is key to building a sustainable and lasting relationship.

2. He's worth it if he notices your undone shoe laces, then bends down to tie your shoe laces for you on his own. That's a sweet gesture, almost priceless in today's society.

3.   He's worth it if he cooks for you and even offers to clean up after the two of you are done with the meal, that's simply amazing and boy are you one lucky gal!

4.   He's worth it if he holds your hand
     whenever the two of you're in public
     and he has no qualms proudly showing
     others that you're his partner.

5.   He's worth it if he invites you to meet his family, close buddies and colleagues and introduces you as his other half happily.

6. He's worth it if he squeezes toothpaste on your toothbrush every morning or places a glass of water by your bedside every evening to quench your thirst in the middle of the night should you wake up. What a sweetie he is!

7.   He's worth it if he fetches you to work and picks you up after work without complaints, and preferably with a smile on his face when he sees you. He cares for you deeply.

8. He's worth it if he takes the time to listen to you, i.e. he puts aside whatever he's doing at that moment and pays total attention to you when you talk.

9. He's worth it if he initiates and talks about a future with you once your relationship has stabilized and you've grown much closer together.

10. He's worth it if he doesn't fight with you for the blanket or bolster, or even if he does, he relents and lets you have it.

11. He's worth it if he's willing to make the bed or place the toilet seat down, or bring the trash out, without you having to nag him about it.

12. He's worth it if he tries really hard to buy you a present he thought you would like. His efforts deserve full marks regardless of whether you truly like the gift or not. Be grateful, smile and say thank you sincerely.

13. He's worth it if he likes children and loves taking care and playing with them. Extra brownie points to be awarded if he actually volunteers to take them out for a meal, excursion or change diapers etc. This man's a keeper!

14. He's worth it if he tells you that you're beautiful even when your mascara's smudged and you look terrible. Beauty lies in the eye of the beholder and this beholder's smitten with you!

15. He's worth it if he's willing to make you breakfast so you can sleep more and then serve you in bed, plus do the dishes afterwards. This is a five-star grading!!!

16. He's worth it if he's willing to attend your family functions despite knowing that your family's very dysfunctional and he'll not feel comfortable during those couple of long hours. He really loves you!

17. He's worth it if he comes along for girl-friend dinner dates, school reunions and social get-togethers without coming up with tricks or lousy excuses to avoid attending. And he doesn't pull a long face during those events.

18. He's worth it if he agrees to watch movies or plays or attend concerts, which he's not a fan of but you love, at least three times a year.

19. He's worth it if he believes it's important for you to have your own personal and financial independence plus social life even though you're a couple. He's a wise man!

20. He's worth it if he thinks of you and your welfare before making any important decisions. He respects you a lot and you're integral in his life.

21. He's worth it if he discusses important matters or issues with you. This shows he values your opinion and respects you. Priceless!

22. He's worth it if he gives you massages when you feel tired and foot rubs, especially when you're pregnant with his child. Your man's such a gem!

23. He's worth it if he automatically buys two portions of foods, knowing there's no dinner at home that evening. And he's brilliant if he happens to buy your favorite foods!

24. He's worth it if he bothers to keep himself healthy. He obviously can't bear to leave you alone before both of you reach your eighties together.

25. He's worth it if he cares for your parents, siblings and relatives. His love for you is that great and he knows they're important people in your life.

26. He's worth it if he keeps you smiling and feeling contented on most days. This is a smart guy who knows that a happy partner / wife makes a happy union and life.

27. He's worth it if he buys you things you love. He actually bothers to remember your likes or he bothers to ask your best friend what you like prior to buying. What an awesome man!

28. He's worth it if he leaves the last piece of chocolate or candy for you to enjoy. He's sweet and very considerate, especially towards you!

29. He's worth it if he lets you sob on his shoulder and cry buckets on his favorite shirt because you had a bad day or needed a good cry.

30. He's worth it if he respects your faith or religion or better still, shares the same faith and values as you.

31. He's worth it if he is polite to servers
     at restaurants, and service staff at
     theatres, stadiums, shops etc.

32. He's worth it if he's ambitious, responsible and works hard to provide for you and the family.

33. He's worth it if he's honest with you and his words are gold. These are invaluable traits!

34. He's worth it if he tells you his deepest fears or darkest secrets. He obviously trusts you with his vulnerabilities!

35. He's worth it if he makes time for you regardless of how busy his schedule is. He values you as his partner!

36. He's worth it if he always makes sure of your safety when both of you're out in the streets, along stairways or in dangerous situations etc.

37. He's worth it if he's generous with you.
     In his mind, his hard earned money's
     meant to be shared with or showered
     upon you, lucky girl!

38. He's worth it if he holds your hand often, in the car while driving, strolling at the park, in the theatre etc.

39. He's worth it if he lets you nag at him because he knows he deserves it and something's still not done.

40. He's worth it if he endures your 'bitchy' behavior because it's that time of the month and you're feeling terrible. He's a gem if he makes you a pot of chamomile tea or feeds you chocolates ☺

41. He's worth it if you come home drunk and he cleans you up nicely and reproaches you gently about not doing it again because it's dangerous for a woman to be that drunk out by herself. Wow, wow, wow, you have to love this guy!

42. He's worth it if he's totally understanding when you need to go off for a girls' getaway and it is at short notice. He truly wants you to have your own social life and a good time.

43. He's worth it if he enjoys talking to you about any and everything under the sun. The two of you can converse for hours and have a good chuckle in between. Girl, lock up your gem of a man!

44. He's worth it if he enjoys a rousing discussion with you because you're two unique individuals and have differing perspectives on issues. More importantly, he doesn't force his opinions on you.

45. He's worth it if he allows you to win some arguments because he knows keeping peace in the family's more important than winning trivial fights. Smart man!

46. He's worth it if he praises your cooking despite parts of the meat being overcooked and vegetables too limp. He loves you a lot!

47. He's worth it if he puts his pride aside and places you first because you matter more during arguments or in certain situations. Keep him for life!

48. He's worth it if he honors his promises to you, big or small. Nothing says more than a man who makes efforts instead of being all talk and no action.

49. He's worth it if he's there to feed your children, bathe them, read them stories at bedtime and tuck them in bed willingly.

50. He's worth it if he's usually the one to apologize first, or buys you flowers after a cold war or fight even though he may not be the one at fault. This man's fabulous!

51. He's worth it if he sets a date night every month after marriage and three kids because he knows keeping the romance alive between the two of you is the key to a successful union.

52. He's worth it if he recognizes that you're better at managing finances and gives you access to all his assets for you to manage. What a wise man!

53. He's worth it if he encourages you to chase after your dream and supports you wholeheartedly even if some sacrifices will have to be made affecting both of you.

54. He's worth it if he lets you climax first every time you make love. This man's so selfless and his love for you is boundless, lock him up and throw the key away!

55. He's worth it if he doesn't have a roving eye whether you're next to him or not. It's one thing to visually appreciate good looking women with no feelings attached but another to lust after them constantly.

56. He's worth it if he encourages you when you're feeling down and chides you when you're behaving poorly. This man's a good influence on you!

57. He's worth it if he's genuine and authentic when he's with you. A real man doesn't need to pretend to be who he isn't.

58. He's worth it if he makes time and tries his best to socialize with your close friends and attempts to get accepted by them because he knows they're important to you.

59. He's worth it if he remembers all
the dates that matter to you—your
birthday, anniversary, Valentine's Day,
Christmas, your parents' and siblings'
birthdays, children's birthdays etc.

60. He's worth it if he buys or brings you a small gift when he returns from his trip every time. It's not about how much the present costs, it's more about him thinking of you even from afar.

61. He's worth it if he tells you his feelings, shows his gratitude or mentions that he loves you often. He's being very honest, open and caring with you and this is amazing!

62. He's worth it if you feel that he respects you as his equal or his partner when the two of you're alone or with company. It's critical for any union to have mutual respect, especially in relationships.

63. He's worth it if he's not offended or disgusted or worse, embarrassed of you (or better still laughs with you) when you fart, burp or vomit alone with him or in public. Two thumbs up for this dude!

64. He's worth it if he calls you when he says that he'll call you. He has a genuine interest in you and specially makes time for you.

65. He's worth it when he arrives early or on time for dates with you. That's sincerity and flattery rolled into one manly package!

66. He's worth it when he is not bothered by your bulging tummy, love-handles, cellulite or acne. This guy's not shallow!

67. He's worth it if he bothers to take up your hobby too so that he can spend more time with you.

68. He's worth it if he opens the doors for you and remembers his basic manners with you and others. What a gentleman!

69. He's worth it if he does small gestures of love and shows concern for you often. He's someone who knows how to cherish you.

70. He's worth it if he looks after you when you're ill. He's someone who can be there to look after you when you need him. Extra points if he cooks and cleans for you too!

71. He's worth it if he doesn't make you feel let down (often). It's important to be with someone who uplifts you rather than suck the life out of you.

72. He's worth it if he inspires and makes you want to be a better human being. This world's made more beautiful with people like him who can inspire others.

73. He's worth it if he stands by you and stays with you even after witnessing your worst behavior. He's someone whom you can count on at your lowest point in life who'll not desert you.

74. He's worth it if he knows what you are thinking by the look in your eyes or a gesture. This is priceless!

75. He's worth it if he works very hard just to buy you something you've always wanted or he knows it's really important to you.

76. He's worth it if he shares the same sense of humor with you. Life's so much more fun and enjoyable when you can laugh a lot with the one you love.

77. He's worth it if he has similar key moral values and life principles as you. This means lesser arguments and unnecessary friction between the two of you.

78. He's worth it if he's willing to go the extra mile for you. His love for you is bigger than whatever additional efforts he needs to put in for you.

79. He's worth it if he treats you in a special manner compared to others and people notice it as well. This man's awesome!

80. He's worth it if he doesn't mind your past, accepts and loves your present and looks forward to a future with you.

81. He's worth it if he's not physically, emotionally or mentally abusive to you or anyone else. Otherwise, run as fast as you can!

82. He's worth it if he remembers your likes and dislikes plus favorites. What a fantastic guy!

83. He's worth it if he puts thought into buying presents for you, whether he gets it right or wrong.

84. He's worth it if he remembers to call when he goes overseas, upon landing and before departing, because he knows you'll worry otherwise.

85. He's worth it if he calls you every night because he wants to hear your voice or talk to you even if it's just for a minute. Two thumbs up!

86. He's worth it if he laughs or at least smiles at your corny jokes knowing you tried your best to entertain him.

87. He's worth it if he automatically does the heavy chores because he wouldn't want you to over-exert or hurt yourself. How caring of him!

88. He's worth it if you lose a shoe and there's another mile to walk so he piggybacks or carries you or gives you his shoes to wear. This man deserves a big kiss!

89. He's worth it if he wants to take responsibility and marry you when you get pregnant and doesn't ask you to go for an abortion.

90. He's worth it if he's the hunter in the dating process or at least bothers to woo you some. Otherwise, he'll take you for granted really quickly.

91. He's worth it if he still sees you as his
beloved and precious girl 10, 20, 30
years down the road together. This guy
recognizes the diamond in you!

92. He's worth it if he loves you more than his car or bank account. This is important because money should never be valued more than you.

93. He's worth it if the two of you get into an accident and he asks whether you're hurt first before he checks his car.

94. He's worth it if he brings out the best in you and you know you're a better person now than the old you.

95. He's worth it if you feel beautiful and confident when you're with him. This will ensure a more sustainable relationship.

96. He's worth it if you feel more vibrant and hopeful towards life compared to before. His presence adds more joy and positivity.

97. He's worth it if you feel safe and secure next to him. This will allow for longevity in your relationship.

98. He's worth it if you feel super contented and happy. Feeling good's what keeps your soul happy and your body healthy.

99. He's worth it when he's respectful to the elders and willingly looks after the younger ones in your family. He'll make a great father to your children.

100. He's worth it if he notices when your hands get cold or you look ill and then takes good care of you till you get well.

101. He's worth it because he's in your life and you thank God every day for this. It's as simple as that!

A Letter To The Worthy You:

Hey Girl,

Thanks for finishing this book ☺

Do me a favor and spend another five minutes with me before you close and put this book down. First of all, take a deep breath now. Take another deep breath. And take one more please. I hope you feel better now than you did a while ago.

The most important thing for you to remember is that you are very much loved! God loves you. The Universe loves you. I love you (my dear reader ☺). Your family loves you. Your friends love you. Your pet loves you. You should love yourself more!

You, my dear, are so blessed! You have an abundance of love to tap into. So do not ever think that a man's love is the be all and end all. NEVER let a man's love be the sole reason behind your happiness. Your happiness is not dependent on a man and that is a real fact. Until you truly understand this vital knowledge, you will forever be dancing to his tune and your life revolving around his.

Often we may be in a situation where we feel confused about where we stand with our partners. We wonder if the relationship is worth holding on to, or if he is worthy of your love etc. So, know this, the answer is actually already within you or at the very least, it will come to you very soon from your subconscious to the conscious.

The actions detailed in this book are from real-life good men. And there are many of such men around us. The difference and bottom line is he is worth it if he is willing to do those things especially for YOU. And if your man is already doing them, then congratulations girl, you have found a worthy one to keep.

I wish you the best of luck in being with one such man in your life. Even if your current man does not do all of the 101 things, if he does a few and those few are the ones which matter to you, then it is your call.

Be wise, my dear. Do not delude yourself, do not make excuses for him, and do not be the one to explain his actions or inaction. It is your life and YOU matter, so please cherish yourself and be happy.

It is sometimes better to be alone than to be with someone who is not worthy of you. Being with someone and still feeling lonely is scarier than being alone. As long as you like your own company, then fret not.

Have more faith, summon more of that inner strength and believe. Believe in yourself, God or The Universe and trust that you are worth it! Enjoy and shine on, girl! Peace be with you, always!

With lots of love,

Wendt Francoise